T0145995

AN ALCHEMIST WITH ONE EYE ON FIRE

CLAYTON ESHLEMAN

an alchemist with one eye on fire

BLACK WIDOW PRESS

BOSTON, MASS.

AN ALCHEMIST WITH ONE EYE ON FIRE
CLAYTON ESHLEMAN

BLACK WIDOW PRESS is an imprint of
Commonwealth Books, Inc., Boston
JOSEPH S. PHILLIPS, Publisher
www.blackwidowpress.com

All Black Widow Press books are printed on
acid-free paper in sewn and glued bindings.

Design and composition by Quemadura
Printed in the United States on acid-free,
recycled paper by Thomson-Shore

ISBN-13: 978-0-9768449-5-2
ISBN-10: 0-9768449-5-8

Library of Congress Cataloging-in-Publication Data
Eshleman, Clayton.
An alchemist with one eye on fire /
Clayton Eshleman. — Black Widow Press ed.
p. cm.
Includes bibliographical references.
ISBN-13: 978-0-9768449-5-2 (alk. paper)
I. Title.
PS3555.S5A43 2006
811'.54—dc22
2006023924

CONTENTS

■

My heart pounded Take Heed!
halfway up the mountain to Chauvet's entrance.
Alarmed to almost be ended
within minutes of the cave—

                    Breathe &
        be grateful for the various ranges
quilted within, & the many years
        with Caryl,   thoughts of her
on that mountainside,   panting—

Did her devotion & utter decency
        lift me on?

[MONTELIMAR, RELAIS DE L'EMPEREUR,
8 JANUARY 2004, 3:30 P.M.]

AN ALCHEMIST WITH ONE EYE ON FIRE

AN ALCHEMIST WITH
ONE EYE ON FIRE

N. O. Brown: "The central feature of the human situation is the existence of the unconscious, the existence of a reality of which we are unconscious." Poetry, then, is about the extending of human consciousness, making conscious the unconscious, creating a symbolic consciousness that in its finest moments overcomes all the dualities in which the human world is cruelly and eternally, it seems, enmeshed.

Part of being fully human is to realize that one is a metaphor. To be a metaphor is to be hybrid, or as Arthur Rimbaud put it, to have a "marvelous body." The first poets were those Upper Paleolithic people who, apprehending that their brothers and sisters were separating the animal out of their heads, and projecting it onto cave walls, attempted to rebond with the animal. These proto-shamans depicted themselves with animal and bird heads, creating a grotesque (initially of the grotto) in which there was symbolic communication between the new human and the old animal realms. Under Rimbaud chasing black and white moons during a Paris hashish session is a young Cro-Magnon dreaming of fiery horses zooming in and out of the sky in a cave somewhere in what would become southwestern France thousands of years later.

In the work of certain poets—William Blake, Lautréamont, H.D., Hart Crane, Antonin Artaud, and Allen Ginsberg come immediately to mind—an archaic and symbolic reality is present. In Artaud's case, the shamanic elements are particularly striking. His vision quests to northern Mexico and southwestern Ireland, use of a magic dagger and cane, loss of identity, possession by doubles, appearing to die during electroshock, glossolalia, spitting, the projection of magical daughters from his own body, and his imaginative resurrection in the Rodez asylum, have more to do with shamanism than with the lives of nineteenth- and twentieth-century "men of letters." What is devastatingly absent in the Artaud scenario is a supporting community. Artaud is a Kafka man, putting himself through a transfiguring self-initiation to discover, stage by stage (until the final two years of his life), that he was regarded by his fellow men as an obnoxious and dangerous pariah.

We live in the age of the death of eternity, the age of mortal sky, ocean, and earth, with such caves as Lascaux, Niaux, and Chauvet today appearing to be the cemeteries of the Cro-Magnon paradise. From the Tang Dynasty to Modernism, poets, in spite of the never-ending terror of so-called "mother nature," have sought refuge in a vision of the impermanent permanent. In spite of their almost weightless impermanence, they have felt that their writing was underwritten by "something" that would always be, call it gods, eternal recurrence, or the chain of being. Today, wilderness and nature at large have become increasingly insular. Mother nature has become man's problem child—we must now take care of her. And the nuclear bomb is not the only repository for contemporary terror. In 2002, Adrienne Rich wrote me: "I think that modernity itself drives people into terror and hence into presumed certitudes of tribalism, fundamentalism, their concomitant patriarchalism, and even suicidalism (I think of Ariel Sharon as a kind of suicide bomber for his nation, which he is willing to destroy rather than to accept a non-military solution)."

At the turn of the twentieth century, American poetry, with the compelling exceptions of Walt Whitman and Emily Dickinson, was still filled with

Victorian decorum and was a poetry of taste, on extremely limited subjects, written almost exclusively by white males. At the millennium, this picture has changed radically: written by African-American, Asian, Chicano, as well as white heterosexual and declared homosexual men and women, American poetry, as a composite force, has become more representative of humanity.

This democratization of poetry must be evaluated in the light of some three hundred undergraduate and graduate university degree programs offering majors in writing poetry and fiction. This system is now producing thousands of talented but unoriginal writers, most of whom would not be writing at all if it were not for jobs. Once upon a time, there was a "left bank" and a "right bank" in our poetry: the innovative vs. the traditional. Today the writing scene resembles a blizzard on an archipelago of sites. Not only has the laudable democratization of poetry been compromised by being brick-layered into the academy but with few exceptions there is a lack of strong "signature" and a tacit affirmation of the bourgeois status quo, the politics of no politics.

It is as if a new purgatory, a postmodernist DMZ has insinuated itself between the poet and the events of the world. This purgatory is multifaceted and loaded with funhouse mirrors. While it is scrambled with lies, distortions, and the unreported, it is also permeated with global information on a scale undreamed of before the Vietnam War. In the Gulf War, "impersonal force" was presented as a video game, intercut with information-screened press conferences. Today main stream reportage has suppressed the havoc we are wreaking on Iraq. So one goes online to view cadavers in Baghdad morgues.

Exposed to the non-information avalanche generated throughout a country whose interventionist tentacles are coiling about all parts of the globe, the tendency of many poets of all ilks (especially those with a job at stake) is to preoccupy themselves with word games, displays of self-sensitivity, or pastiches of entertaining asides. In the official verse culture backed by *The New Yorker*, *The New York Review of Books*, *The Nation*, and *The New York Times* (magazines and newspapers which often engage current events, history and culture from a liberal point of view), poetry reviews and contributions are determined by taste, precious intellectuality, and a conservative old boys club (which includes old girls). X may be exposed but only under certain conditions and in certain decorous ways. There is still something in the Puritan shallows of the American editor that says: do not attempt to investigate. And do not propose material that does not elicit a knee-jerk reaction, but does require a thoughtful (and often not immediate) response.

What might a responsible avant-garde in poetry today include?

1] Radical, investigational writing that is raw, often wayward, in process; poetry as an intervention within culture against static forms of knowledge, schooled conceptions, clichéd formulations.

2] Writing that evinces a thoughtful awareness of racism, imperialism, ecological issues, disasters, and wars.

3] Multiple levels of language—the arcane, the idiomatic, the erudite, the vulgar, the scientific; relentless probing; say anything; not just "free speech" but *freed speech*.

4] Transgression, opening up of the sealed sexual strong rooms; inspection of occult systems for psychic networks; the archaic and the tribal viewed as part of everyone's fate.

5] Treating boundaries like stage scenery.

I look out of my workroom window: redbud tree, neighbor's garage, church parking lot, gray Michigan winter sky. Bland, peaceful. When I first drafted this essay in 2002, I saw an Afghani woman in full body veil sitting on a bridge in Kabul, begging. She was in a Taliban frame, one constructed in large part by the CIA which helped create Osama Bin Laden. After bombed Afghanistan reverted back to warlord-controled regionalism, as the second act in the same play, "mission accomplished" Iraq has become a cemetery for at least 40,000 of its citizens, under a rain of 500-pound bombs and 127 tons of depleted uranium munitions. What the Bush administration would have Americans believe was a double reaction to the 9/11 assault now appears to have been in planning stages for not only years but as a program of global domination (taking over from England, now our junior neo-colonial partner) set forth at the end of World War II.

As a citizen of a country that has supported such terrorists as the Nicaraguan Contras, UNITA in Angola, the Moujahedeen in Afghanistan, Cuban CIA agents in Miami, and the governments of El Salvador, Guatemala, and Chile, the American poet reaps and suffers the rewards of American terrorism, which are part of his spectre, his anti-imaginative blockage, whether he acknowledges such or not. All of us are connected to the rubble of Fallujah by a poisoned umbilicus.

Unlike poets in China, Iran, and Nigeria, I can still say anything I want to say (for a while at least). This is not only suspect freedom—it renders my situation absurd. I am like a maniac allowed to wander about screaming "fire" in a theater of the deaf. Am I a traitor? Certainly not. I am not committed to the overthrow of anyone or anything. I remind myself mostly of a late–nineteenth-century alchemist mixing and cooking my potions in a

Prague apartment—an alchemist with one eye on fire from what he knows is going on outside his laboratory.

As a middle-class American, I am overexposed to the front side of our avuncular top-hatted Uncle Sam. Much of the world has a different view of Sam than I do. Iraqis, Serbs, Laotians, Vietnamese, Cambodians, and Panamanians, for example, see a skeletal backside wired with DU, cluster bombs, dioxin, sarin, napalm (most recently used in Fallujah), and hydrogen cyanide. I know what I see and I keep both sides of Sam's body in mind as I continue to work on myself, to learn, and to love. I show nearly everything that I write to my wife, Caryl. She reads it, tells me what she thinks. Intelligent and honest, she knows my writing well and sometimes detects its flaws. After we talk, I do more work and make more flaws! This exchange is one of the reasons that, at seventy, I continue to write—poetry as a space that two people can enter and relate through. A small world. But no smaller than the human universe, which is a match flicker in cosmic night.

Where is poetry going today? To hell, as usual—not to Christian Hell, but to the underworld, to our pre-Christian unconscious, which is pagan and polytheistic. Poetry's perpetual direction is its way of ensouling events, of seeking the doubleness in events, the event's hidden or contradictory meaning. The first poets, facing the incomprehensible division between what would become culture and wilderness, taught themselves how to span it and thus, momentarily, to be whole in a way that humankind could not be whole before it became aware of its differences from animals.

American poets today, facing the possibly comprehensible mindset of neocon conquest, *amor-fati*, and the need to find out for oneself, must assimilate such vectors and figure out ways to articulate them. If we cannot accomplish this, then our distinction may become that of being the first generation to have lived at a time in which the origins and the end of poetry became discernable.

I continue to regard poetry as a form in which the realities of the spirit can be tested by critical intelligence, a form in which the blackness in the heart of man can be confronted, in which affirmation is only viable when it survives repeated immersions in negation—in short, a form that can be made responsible for all the poet knows about himself and his world.

NOCTURNAL VEILS

In bed, looking up at the light-peppered dark,
as if the ceiling were not there, as if I were staring into
my own staring. Tinctured absence. A grassy sweet aroma
    lifting off Caryl.
                      In the zone between
here and not here, the lunar curtain parts,
as in a Matta painting, there are tilting astro-planes,
each a kind of ark, or flight deck,
one covered with snow has standing mammoths—it tilts,
slides through a plane crawling with reptiles.
I think of my brain with its reptile stem, its mammal hood,
I see a bear humping a crocodile,
try to get between them, to push them apart, open a space for a nascent self.
In the zone between bear and crocodile, what will I be?
A bear-headed croco-boy? A croc-headed baby bear?
I screw off my head, toss it into the dark
—will it become a raven? A large bee?
Headless, I watch through my chest the air swarming with spirits,
Nora! How is it where you are?
"Busy. Bodies rushing in and out, did you know Cheney is full of reptile blood,
and driven by the mind of an Incan child abandoned on a mountain
300 years ago? A child spitting up
lizard blood, freezing to death in a stone shrine,
now can you grasp Cheney's infantile wrath?
Bush's secret is his tiny tail, leathery, about 3 inches,
like the tip of a Komodo Dragon's tail—

note how he is always heavily guarded from behind,
for if some joker pulls his tail, a long yellow forked tongue will spurt from
    his face—
very few humans are pure human, most are occupied by
bizarre creature combines, the dead and the extinct pack the air
unseen from a senses-five perspective.
I have a horse's cock now, and I'm planning on using it soon,
I'm going to fuck one of those dead art dealers
who "fucked" me, then help her open a gate to your plane,
watch the fun as she gives birth in a few brains to some mustang raillery!"

She screamed with laughter—then I heard a strong, central suck,
something in the dark had gulped her back.

The pepper-dotted room began to undulate.
I thought of the veils within "No one has lifted her veil,"
    revelation, to draw back the *velum*,
to hear dead Nora through a spiritual gate,
to see the Dogon earth naked and speechless,
without language, a fiber skirt the first word,
speech as plaited fiber, "speech lattice,"
or Christ nailed on the cross as the arrested word,
vulva as lower mouth issuing red fiber,
a many-colored Isis rainbow, net within which
my fate is entangled, where the Nora spirits can be heard.

Then I saw a black-capped facial netted "full body veil"
sitting, as if on the Kabul bridge, begging.
"No one has lifted her veil" became

"At no time have women not been oppressed."
My heart tore left and right, I tried to peel
the true from the truthful, the rainbow flashed
a central scarlet band—I knew it was the Wawilak Sisters' menstrual blood
circulating within rock python venom.
I saw ripples of albino babies, each with a red or silver balloon,
setting off across the rainbow bridge for
the argentine body of the moon—

the Kabul bridge beggar roared back,
burkha, menstrual never shed,
chrysalis of a monstrous anti-metamorphosis
"sewed up in a hammock, with a small opening so she can breathe"
—are all of us, enclosed in the world of five senses, mummified pupas?
The beggar hissed: "Your bars, spaced and wall-papered, allow some
    comfort and expanse.
Mine, wrapped around me, nearly cover my eyes . . ."

I turned and sought sleep's stagnation,
respite from the sear of intersecting planes.

PAUSE

I hear you close the bathroom door.

An absence-weighted balance lifts into presence.

Is the source of human bondage the fear of loss?

Now that you are showering, cables of water convert, ghost-loaded
    suds, Rabelais's mane furls from Aphrodite's thigh . . .

The patter of my tattered tale, swirled drain. Rising like a sewer
    of precognition: Is the real death the death I am preoccupied with
    here and now?

The sound of drying, the clay in the cloth, the veil that will rend me
    before I reach the end.

To pull out the last part of myself left inside, to get all of myself
    born.

LIFE IN THE FOLDS

Imagination has never met a non-love it did not love,
or a wall with which it did not become engaged.
I am a convict of light in the suction panic of the sun.
The range is eternity, the focus? The halter of time—
a babe in halter we spring up and down,
restrained, eternity invades our dreams,
spreads across the stone, form trancing form.
What is is inherent in what is not.
Only in the abyss do time and eternity
dissolve into a sinless source of origin.
The first image was a prompter box, gesturing to
an us spread out like bat wings on
a stone relief. Each second is
vertical with middened hives,
I fish for bait trapped in my own line.
Across the stone, the actor hordes are
streaming ochre, enmassed manganese penetrates
their menstrual pour. The tunnel is enlightenment if
death's lager can be drunk there.
Silo hide, imprisoned sand
course my throat, an appled road rent
with all who have responded to daybreak's
roll call of bones.

In the suction panic of the sun, we are
entwisted spectres, our veins streaming with verdure,
octopodal bursts of infant flowers,
tender calcium—in your
outstretched hand you hold our wheat,
in your torso interior a banquet hall collapses,
a Lethe seeping into mist-dead-dusk.
In comparison, all retwists—I watch
a watch-headed serpent enter your red breast-hung hall—
on the same mobius strip we act,
via awareness of death, as if we are alone.
Your head disappeared eons ago—
my tombal shoulders, armless, dimming with
sallow orchards, writhe stilly
as your charge bolts and
makes beaver shapes in Matta's mind. I spot him
at the horizon's vortex where the panic hits
and the sun takes on stick insect latitude, filmy cosmic trestle
before which we bend and whisper,
green fuses trapped in a summons that runs
through the known, now picking up coprolites of
uncharted waste.

I participate, in advance, in future time.
My point of reference is spherical, amoebic,
a choir of strings. I take my leads from
tunnel intestinal macaroni, ancestor lines
wandering, having left their rear-ending hole

—no one has touched bottom!
Bottom is a hole made from the speed of engendering poles.
The jungle holds up a mirror, we see we are chalk
traceries in outer space, grasped briefly
as elves, under *amanitas*, in the garden of
steel-infested self. Traceries where armored
gnomes slash at menstrual slits.
This raspberry is flooding my mind,
a head of yellow breasts is wearing a Pieta wig.
I set it aside to make way for
an automobile sprouting towers of enraged Iraqis,
derricks of vegetal steam, they wave in and out of view.
I press no button
but I'm American through and not through.
My mind is a jet engine suctioning imperial drift,
attempting to register
an allegiance to dehumanized Palestinians
as well as to the Daughters of Energy still viable at
Le Combel. Matta now reveals himself:
red disk painted limestone with a vulvar fold
perpendicular through his being.
A jump cut, he is a flayed dog head studying
a vagina on fire—its soot
surges through an amber emporium of astral scree.
It is the profound and beautiful
femininity of the earth always under man attack.
I crawl toward the mirage of an Aurignacian candelabra
still glistening with cosmic dive.

I eat a leech and watch its Whitmanian suckers unfold
This is wholeness,
or, as close as I'll ever get to a closure
packed with the rubble of
rhinocerotic metonomy.

[PARIS, JUNE 2004]

STILL

Paola at 49 today
trying to focus
as if through mythological mayhem—

Your eyes in squint
your Isinsquint
hearing earrings mirrorings roarings

Your eyeing us through Dionysus,
your one-eye-at-a-time tender smile,
the ghost of Paola vying with
Paola's courage

Through mind din   your eyes
     at half-mast

The soul pouring into invisible mortar.

■

Reduced,
you evoke your bubbling assertions,
your verve, your flair,
your initial suspicion that I worshipped the devil,
the glissando in your laugh,
your bolting after the deer to see the deer bolt,

your smart curiosity,
your love for Bob.

■

In my subconscious,
the germ of your soul is now moon-borne.
If the moon consists of the dead,
your soul germ is now entering the moon's great white back,
this back always turned toward us
as the sun always faces us—
a winged thistle, this soul germ, a fairy-like, magnetized
rush into white self-abandon
where the souls of millions will flock about it, covering it.
What looks like craters are intense mills,
grindstones of the dead, milling new souls,
polishing them to utter extinction, until infinity shows through.

Once an aperture for infinity,
your soul will break free, returning to earth to
enter the psyches of living individuals,
so that for us to sense soul is to sense depth,
a richness of life contingent upon loss,
the presence of moon-milled souls
sinking pits into our shadows,
revealing the lineaments of a totality.

■

Paola, is your soul standing behind this interstice?

I see you in American English
but I sense you in something as old as post-glacial ice,
the power of a presence dimmed by death
but not extinguished, perhaps more present now,
as a presence, because your contours have come undone,
and your size, previously appearing to be physical,
now in dispersal   invests everything with potent absence—

You are more like a woods than an entity,
a woods with its own resurrectional chaos,
with its green Persephonal cycling, as if all the dead,
returning to the fermentative still of the dark,
took the green with them each autumn, and, curious about us,
brought it back each spring.

So you are singular and multiple in a new way now,
a stranger to either/or,
unlike us undivided,
before as well as *behind* the interstices of our hesitant imaginations.

Give us the power to invent a world in which you are a presencial part.
We, the living, at conception marked for death.
You, the dead, pervading our conception of what it is to be.
Do we cross each other?
Are we kissing as we cross?

[IN MEMORIAM PAOLA VALSANIA, AUGUST 2003]

IRISH JIG

Nanosounds,
interior stellar
zoom,
      zoas of
the poetic art,
ecstasy enstacy of
the gyrosonic
    body.

      How I dig it, in fact,
I am a digger wasp on Tyler Duncan's hand, watching him swingle
sound flax out of bagpiped hip,
I enter the wasp nest sound swirl,
merry lines limbically entwine (first parents with long, dragon-
    coiling tails):

spicy early thriller, a sly
pricey thrill, reply as icy thriller, really
tip her lyrics, rip rectally sly heir, rectally
reply Irish, rarely hysteric pill, really
rich piles try, layers prey till rich, rich till
slayer prey, arty lisper rich yell, yell arty
rich perils, lechery rarity pills, thrill
creepy lay sir, slyly retire rich pal, icy

thriller replays, a silly triple cherry, irately
cherry spill, prey ill slithery arc, prey
later silly rich, prey alter rich silly,
slyly rich April tree.

Jig, dyadic Kundalini
    "Caryl Phyllis Reiter"
anagrammatic manger.

Before I was Clayton, I was clan toy, lacy ton, ant cloy,
    any colt,
Rounding thrill icy corners, my face accordion unfolds,
    what twins are spotted
in its pleats! Tunnels of Tezcatlipóca turning plumed—
    archaic sounds,
a maze of reeds, each repeat sprouts new flutings—
    so dart in, retrace,
pivot to reoccur. The obstetrical toad is
gigging in his fertilized skirt.
             Fetal propellers are
turning left, strengthening
    energies into a heart.

YANTRA

The first sound I ever made,
when will it end?
Am I still unpacking it?
Crimson round suitcase
out of which
clothed salamanders drift.
Did I evolve out of sound, out of a lip
    to nipple
triple hiss?
A sound whose sides are space?
Were all straight lines once semi-circled points?
Brown square root vase
out of which
a human head elongates to a snake.
Was I fed by sound?
Is my more than infant shape
a sound stacked armature
about which
my emptiness presses,
a placental cloud?
Are all our sounds traveling out and out,
is the agony of Rwanda
a rash in the stratosphere?

[FOR STEVE BERG]

AN ENIGMATIC SIGNIFIER

My mother is no longer making sense.
She called last dream, garbled and hung up.
At 67, I have passed where her eternity is clear. She who did not
possess the code, encoded me.
What I am missing is encoded in her mice.

When I was hungry, daddy would hold
my kitty mamma up by her front paws.
In her black furry belly there were mouse heads,
one of which I would take
between my hands and put its nose into my mouth.
As I filled up, I saw blue butterflies,
green buds. Around what kind of Eden
did I have my mouth?

One day when kitty mamma did not come,
I cried, and daddy brought out mother.
Had he hid kitty mamma? Mother
had no mouse, mother had
Carnation milk, Kepler cod-liver oil.
Mother daddy would poke at me and laugh:
"does the cat have your tongue?"

What were mice doing
in kitty mamma's body? Were they
trying to emerge? What else was trying

to emerge? What had I
emerged from?

"Tell us how a star goes." Twinkle tinkle twinkle.
"Tell us how a dog." Wow-wow.
Dite   (light)
Chur   (picture)
Dad-da car.
      Her exhausted face
      urging out words.

Suck thumb suck thumb no tinkle suck thumb.
Night and day you are a thumb
in the roaring traffic glare
amongst the pillows of my tiny lair
I suck thumb. Then they tied a thumb-stall on.
Stating *Bok old Mamma*
            Tak-a new Mamma very loud,
I showed my kitty mamma mouse fanged
farce-fed mouth to the world.

LAURA

Caryl and I once drove to northside Indianapolis to visit two high school friends of mine. "We've planned something special for you this afternoon," Nancy Whitaker said. "We're going to drive you around and show you where our old classmates used to live."

James Hillman: "A recent statistic revealed that one third of all adult males in the United States, and one quarter of all adult women would choose to stay *permanently* at the ages between fifteen and nineteen: a life sentence to high school.

Is it high school? Is that what the soul wants, or does it long for something that fifteen to nineteen represents?

The soul longs for the torment of early beauty, for which high school is a stand-in."

Dancing with Ann Jones, 1952, in her Meridian Street penthouse, to "Laura," 52 years later to revisit that violaceous hour, to recognize the hypnosis impacted in "only a dream," underscored by a viola's elegiac tone.

> Is there a Paleo-Laura
> invisibility of a woman for a man
> because of his mother? Does an eternal mother
> reign over
> Laura as a leafless crone
> recycling Persephonic green?

Shuffling in circles to the music,
my palm on her back feels, under the cashmere,
the bra-strap. It hisses in me,
a fuse
planted in a uterine paradise,
word continents pushing up,
crunching into

                  the walled garden
            a teenage diameter away.

SAMPERI'S DIAGRAM

The paradise of the Frank Samperi diagram,
showing poets how to get through. Can you believe it,
I said to Carol Bergé, on the sofa beside me,
she was twisting her hands in something on her lap,
"I am unsure." So I investigated,
spotting the black horse head areas in what looked like
a complex airport diagram, with lights, on a vast wall,
Samperi appeared, more healthy than in life,
"The horse head areas are disaster spots,
you have to figure out how to move around them,"
or did he say "through them?"
                              Now in Samperi's realm,
on his road, or via, I struggled with bales,
saw marvelous living rocks, emerald things speaking to me?
I was in "everything is alive,"
"all is in constant transformation," then I thought of Caryl,
made it back to our bedroom where hunched Samperi figures were by
    her bed, backs to me,
I saw one slithering under the springs,
I threw them away—monks? demons? Samperi outriders?
and immediately wanted to pursue was it Samperi's *Jumanji?*
Not sure, never sure, always on this wavering transcendental road,
    plagued with the iridescent,
where hollows are owls, thrown instantly-sprouting reeds,
reeking with meat, and the meat spills its lore, whore-angels pour,

to reveal the beast in harbor, the hail-spurting storm
    is a chrysanthemum-radiant isle. Then Frank reappeared—
I told him: I'm so blocked by transformation, plus
your henchmen passing rods through Caryl . . .
"Here," Frank said, "work with these . . ."
He spilled some black pebbles which I scooped, swam with,
tossing them before me as I pulsed,
I ran the Samperi road, miles racing under me,
toppled herms, Frank's life and death, I saw the mother he told me was
    a prostitute,
her hair streaming lizards, she wept little Franks who I kissed,
hedges, towers, a rain of moles, a goblet passed or was passed to me,
I watched the shrimp dancing twitch, then drank,
my infancy became a pile of tiny pearls, "what to do" became a lot of tools,
my newspaper route, I was at 49th and Boulevard Place,
freezing, as the truck dumped the Indianapolis Times,
I tore open the moor, to find the under-sage, twiggy trails led me back,
flying Samperi's diagrammatic sentence, I heard
"You've joined the diagram . . ."
                                        Was that Bergé?
"Oh it is wonderful," she said, as I plopped down beside her,
"wonderful when vision works at the speed of mind."
Then I saw her chipmunk, I mean her baby anaconda, and broke down
    in tears:
only parts of the dream could be recovered here, and is this vision?
I have remembered, invented, remember-invented,
I was in paradise how long?
I cannot recall its caul, or its multifoliate delivery—

cannot here recreate the dream's sensual matrix.
This is the real Fall, the divisional void.
Then to awake, face the clock, the media headlock,
what a wrench, fellow man, what a wacky disorienting brainswipe,
the zero time of paradise chopped up into space.

CUL-DE-SAC

Trenchant the chant trench,
the lower valley royal,
trenchant the sound scraping across
subconscious calcification.

Who will descend, verbally,
into the enigmatic signification base?
Who will raise, from bottom logs,
enough mud to shape a new leech?

Don't inquire. Recall, imagine
the womb scree in mother's house-size smile,
your first interior sense
when menstrual flavors invaded the milk.

Arch but be wary, for the serpent, emerging,
is already boring through her right breast
a left-hand path. Attach
yourself to this witch, let her

summon the foul paradise of animal welter,
the six black dots on the terminal wall
are peepholes onto
Coatlicue's war room, where

bloodless men in tall hats are dismembering
Little Red Wombhood and her sisters,
Tinkertoy, Soapdish,
Dada, Twinkle and Prune.

FOR GUSTAF SOBIN

Radiating in my shroud
I governed my matrix
wandering Egyptian *anima mundi*,
sensing in these parent powers
a deeper larval plait.

What was it to see then?
As if with water halfway up one's eyes,
a shimmering miraginality,
breathed blood, non-bioquestioned breath,
walking in carrion-coifed time.

A dimpled slug with rabbit ears.
Equilibrium: cone-shaped loaf, vase of water.
Fecal rainbow undulating through an alabaster jar.
Light entombed in gneiss.
Carnelian amulet. Stromatolithic haystack.

Like you, Gustaf, I've risked wordwreck to excavate
a buried mouth, to release its stumped
root whirl.
                    Every crocodilian kiss
stimulates the soul gown, the veiled animal heads
strutting through our combines.
Stare hard into the atmosphere,

Little Red Riding Hood is there as a rose-colored wolf,
or as an ashen wet-suit
in which, through the smoke hole of the mind,
we shimmy down
our skullracked, sand-blasted
psychic backbone.

LOOKING INTO VERMONT WOODS, AT TINLING'S, OCTOBER 3, 2004

I stepped out to watch leaves, like cobra hoods,
waltzing, wattled parasols.

My eyes, focused latrines—
a purification was under way.

Warm bath of heart re-obtained. To inhale,
to be in the columnar densities of
a warming now taking on global melt.

Leaves as reefs
birch-white with amber pink
    lime-tinted
                Atlas still
the molten under-yolk,
the sphincter of mayhem
Arshile Gorky breathed, staring at gnats adrift,
the grass pun tangents,
                    entry
an ever-exiting bruise,
                    burst
flagellation of a pyre
drummed on by ants,
possessed, in elfin serenade.

Cockscomb and marigold are thistled in
a graphite legacy:
Monody of a line,
Gorky at Pech Merle,
nodal black ballet.
The supped russet totality
eye-needled through.

Nora reappeared last night, in Noh mask,
or, as a Noh mask, halo-negative.
What had happened before was to be realized here.
The poem became a Noh bridgeway
leading to here (the stage) from eternity (the wings).
Art as the great second chance. For who,
in the thick of experience,
is up to her potential imaginative size?

■

"Clayton, climb onto me,
I'll drop you through each painting,
you can shimmy along my wedged-in erections,
those transgressions that made my art despised.
Go, fireman, put on the blaze! Light up the nitwittery
confining you to a senses-five view.
Can't you see your circumference circus fading?
Excuse me, but I have to explode . . .
Mano kuna mako k'olo puti tik aq'ua!
Proto-Nostratic, or in senses-five English:
Man woman child hole vulva finger water.
There's a headless mess from Cougnac here
who claims these words as her own.
Min ma kulkul halok butu paita
tek tik   tika aka waka agua . . .

no word is meaningless, each sound tumbles,
a depth charge, through the creative wiring.
I know you expected me to appear as a goddess,
how fair, really, how fathomable,
but the World Tree is now oil,
there is no Tree other than this dendron talk.
Disappearance is awesome—one moment gust,
one moment   is it absence? We don't have a word,
Heraclitus is foggy,   the soul has an end,
in particulars like oullol, the soul's ends
are   incomprehensible cement-mixers in the living.
Heraclitus was a peasant, as are we all,
when it comes to ridge war . . .
if you and I could only dive into a strawberry . . .
Sailing or spinning, I am full of stones and have no edge . . ."

■

How might I wear you?
As aura, blue larva light
encindered with eyes of the void,
your once precious warmth my cobra shadow,
your mechanic's hand that supped from phalluses,
imbuing your art with man's roan girderwork,
his moray quarrel and hypomania—
or do I bear you in the hyena graveyard
aslant in my dreams, are you
a kind of Kali, tossing
your laughing head from hand to hand?

Is that my spinal tallow spurting from your neck?
Is the most crazed thought possible
here most accurate? Do you entwine my mother,
and if so, are you two kissing
like rattlesnakes erupting from Coatlicue's torso urn?
The energy of the dead has a fetal intensity.
Out of my mouth I give birth to you
as you reposition under my heart.
You are the non-manifest cathecting imagination,
a whirling cross out of which a calf is breaking,
a Xipe-like dream turning me inside out
that I might wear my insides for a moment
and let the outsides rest. No rest
for the anxious non-manifest, this Nora force
on all fours by the well of reindeers,
lapping up turquoise, vomiting beryl.

■

"You are the result of resisting absolute absence
which is what, as non-being, we essentially are.
All our hells, Styxes, fairies and kobolds
are manifestations of what we still cannot face:
non-existence, out of which,
like a hybrid half-alive, existence appears.
Or so it seemed to those, eons before you,
who, knowing nothing about procreation,
saw the vagina as a potential extra-terrestrial gate.
After Hiroshima, the American fear of extra-

terrestrial invasion increased immensely.
Humankind's tragedy is in not living symbolically.
The Fall is into the literal, the failure to accept
that it is the woman who feeds the snake.
Once the shells of the dead
honeycombed the back of the Tree.
Now I peer through your holes,
a hole trolling your holes, which are not holes,
since only the dead own holes . . . well, we do not
own shit,   think of home as abyss gas,
or the god sound of a neck
sliced sandwich bitten into
by the mayor of your own spiritual wreck.
We should only add up in imagination.
Are you aware that what limits energy, makes laws,
practices vengeance, desires domination,
weeps over its victims, creates sin, and then repents
—a Christian-patinaed, self-justifying
carcan of uroboric circling—
is Reason? And it is still part of what is left of me.
But only now do I see its circular causation,
its totaling subtraction."

■

What are you doing this evening?

"I'm evening doing through the what of are."

Meaning?

"Of course, of absence—the meaning lingam hangs, dripping reefers, or rectile amusements. Hard to tell because there is no here or there, only your mind, and mine, a mind mine without walls or fuse."

Do you see me?

"No, I move about you, watery, an air oil, in darkness so dense your heart is a pip I cushion . . . are you alive?

Yeah, I just turned 68, and since you always remembered my birthday . . .

"That was before, when there was a for to be for, when I had a body to incline . . . I can't tell you how it is to exist in absence, and not be able to point, like a dog, to train onto a smell. Did you just eat?"

I don't want to pick on what you've debecome. No, I did not just eat.

"Liar."

How do you know?

"You would probably only listen to me when you are satiated, not in a Harrison state, but hardly sipping a spider with Simone Weil. What we did not see when alive is strictly enforced now."

I made scallops with carmelized ginger, sautéed boiled burdock with tamari and gomasio, and let some steamed dandelion greens warm in basil-scented olive oil . . .

"I can't understand a word of that . . . did you just switch to Proto-Globic?"

No, I described our delicious meal . . .

"Our illicit eel? What are you talking about? Did you know what Joe did to me?"

Yes and no. The huge painting tacked to one wall of your bedroom is the most frightening I have seen. I felt that it was a vision of Joe's presence, his unrelentingly overbearing presence, right over the bed . . .

"Your back is fascinating—why is it so integumental, and iridescent? You told me you're still alive—why do I see folded wings in your back?"

Joe was too much?

"When men stick stuff up you, it smears memory with hallucination. You become obsessed with explaining their phallic bladework, their sky-scrapers, their roto-rooters that turn your sexuality into a Japanese restaurant food display—not that he actually cut me (actually he did). Not that he actually cut (actually . . ."

What does my back look like?

"Mangenta-hued, glossy, the folded wings spotted with black-in-white bull's eyes, or skulls, as if the physical part of you is still in chrysalis, filled with poisonous, frothy blood. There are also bright rings in barber-pole motion around what I take to be your spine, and beings I can't make out.

They say the dead see; we see only partially, we see things you do not see, and we do not see things you see. Now I see an ancient apartment-like complex in your back, levels on which creatures are doing things in garish, unfurnished cells, around your spine, or serpent-tube sprouting tunnels, you seem to be smoking with tunnels, and in one—O no, not Joe . . . O Jesus, not Joe."

Go on, get over Joe.

"Over? Have you studied *under*? As a man, do you know what it is to be under, really under? Call my paintings "Under," the whole erection-latticed maze of them, UNDER. Where were we? In this sirloin blackness you seem to have a goat pelvis, a bone anvil on which something tells me the Medusa is ceaselessly impounded . . . But is it yours? Does anything belong to anyone? O Clayton, for moments I was alive!"

■

The truth of something, yes,
but can the truth of nothing be shown?
Someone touches you in this way:
she opens the car door and you see your double
carrying a fuming censer pass through a smoking gate.
The instant blazes, immediately gone,
and you realize each instant is so fully empty
you allow it to pass, massively, at the speed of
taking it for granted—for isn't it already nothing,
a stone representing the empty fullness of your life?
To drink from each moment, but not to drain,

to taste drily, what a challenge, to live and to unlive
all of one's granted taking every day,
to be here, in the zero of the instant, *of* the instant,
and of that lapse in the instant dreaming creates,
so that one might wake and, if only for moments,
be the headless god of the dreaming-awake mind,
before all the instants are baled and frosted.

■

And how do you see my soul, I asked Nora.

"It looks to be from Arnhem Land,
a greasy red knot with filaments aspiral,
now I see maggots on knuckle-bones,
you were entered by one,
it sank into you a fiery amulet.
Your birth was blank and right-handed,
you're always drizzling or leaking secrets
and you throw out too many loops to the unregenerate.
This ancestor of yours was brought by a German circus to Switzerland,
and exhibited. Before dying of ptomaine poisoning
he mated with a cage-slosher.
The infant was adopted by an Aeschelmann family
who raised the boy to be a veterinarian
specializing in livestock.
While performing a Caesarean section,
he spotted the Virgin's face enwebbed with the fetus
and thereupon renounced earthly labor and delight.

He embalmed the calf fetus and prayed to it,
believing that he had made contact with a nexus uniting
the Virgin with the Beast, an unfortunate association,
for church elders in Bern interpreted this identification as satanic,
proposing that Ira Aeschelmann had delivered
nothing less than the Apocalyptic Whore's fetus.
He was lucky to be merely banished
and spent the remainder of his 77 years
as a kind of wild hermit, wandering the Alps.
Imprint is all. These circuits now
range in your shadow, ankle-chained but lively, constantly skittering
    out of the light."

Nora, did you know American democracy has become "ceramic Roman decay?"

"Worse: 'any ceramic comrade.'"

Anagrams aside, what do we look like from your void of view?

"Bicep-bloated, with millions of skulls dangling from multiple armpits. But why ask about such stuff? Political fester is clearly literal."

If I could have, at the same time, a vision and a bird's eye view of Israel and Palestine, I might grasp something that from an earthly viewpoint seems hopeless.

"Look at that fucking fence the Israelis are building! Are you telling me they are going to tear that down and uproot 200 settlements? This one is ground zero from out here. We like it. You want to know the kernel? It's about the beaten kid who becomes a father and beats his kid. What do you expect the Israelis to do? Shit their horror and become regenerate in a half-dozen generations? Israel is a traumatized conglomerate. They have to extirpate a spectre attached to sonship, and until they do they will lay eggs in the backs of the filial Palestinians—but the suicide bomber is one of ours, one foot in the inexistent, the other in that abysss called faith."

The inexistent?

"Neither non nor ex, but the force out of which you achieved conception. I saw cocks as an X-ray of the twentieth century and I painted them hard, bent, and bandaged, I delivered them in a forest ballet of female contingencies, they appear as stalagmites and ruined ghosts, but appear they do, these previously hidden, enigmatic signifiers, these Prufrock omissions dicing narrative into floating heads and limbs. Gorky and Bellmer were my gate guardians, and here they are tonight, two elegant storms, one on each side of the orifice in which the world buried its hammerhead. Have you forgotten my having told you of my last lover, the one who would remain, in me, motionless for hours? Surely he was the solstice between my womanhood and this inexistence, a mane of shadow flowing, yet still, in the interstice behind each point of existence . . . you were not my vermilion, but you were my beryl, my dear yellow jacket, with your tawny words, dear hub of an other-brother. Now, I'm in vertical fade, my torched astrological houses floating through yours. I'm watching your twins fish in a star stream, little cupids, or beefy gnomes, their lines like descending tentacles of mental war. How strange to feel our identities as huge buildings coming apart, floating wall and floor-wise through each, my mortar, your edging, or is it your angling breaking up with my space.

Dear Nora, you are not a ghost,
you are admittance to
that space where word crickets reknot lewdly,
where the octopus deliveries take place.
Until we cease shifting planes,
let us cross the abyss to each other!
Until we centuplicate always and never,
let us converse!

[APRIL 2003—FEBRUARY 2004]

46

Dick Cheney's mouth
slides on circular-saw teeth, with rakers,
to rip out the throats of words,
to drape their wormcasts,
scare nets, over brains hypnotized by
the blind light of innocence,
that tunnel of camouflaged history called
"it's a free country."

Bush is an enraged grave,
a plutonium bell tolling human clappers.
Bush in exaltation drag
on a Midas-headed corporate beast
centuplicating with the beliefs of Christian reconstructionists,
whose "immortality" is posited on
the extermination of humanistic idolators.

"Who can deny that the use of gunpowder against pagans
is the burning of incense to Our Lord?"

"Cain's right leg was a mangled slab of splintered bone and stringy red
muscle; both knees were visibly dislocated; the left thigh was twisted at a
bad angle, indicating a broken femur, and the leg appeared both seared and
flayed. Cain was shrieking in agony and pain . . . wrapping the 'mush' of the
right leg in bandages, splinting both legs, they rolled Cain on his side and
discovered that his left buttock was half torn-off, the flesh laced with rough
bits of the truck cab."

I have this image of myself that is too
visual,   how bring it into verbal
                    imagination?
how to say myself as an American 21st-century
    exasperated person?
                         Everything seems to be
a dodge,   no,   not a dodge,
an impossible,   my standing before you
with Bush raining through me,   but I'm not
the object,   I'm more the rain,   through the force
    of Bush—

We've entered a period in which words shine
like sunned-on sunglasses
—or are these glasses lensless,
is this shine socket stare?

Francis Bacon's CEOs out of office
are Leon Golub's mercs, out of suit
into jeans with a Kalashnikov girlfriend.
Where once was Eden,
"in the sands of the desert,"
such men re-embed in a predatory self roomy enough
for a gigantomachy to find stage.
Birth gate: boxing ring,
mother columnar legs. She's pushing out
a domed church! Why has she paws?
Why are the fetuses mummified?
Sphinxine pointless and riddled change.

Wound in the shape of man.
The whole stage, man. Nature
ground up in man. Men as self-flayed palookas
bouncing off, running through.
Power so masculinized
true north is another man to kill.

Haze glare, steep
hills rising from villaged shore,
salmon   ochre
    white rambling chesswork
homes broadcast under beveling mist
                    slipping down from
    cloud obscure peaks,
hypodermic needle spire afloat.

Villa set in verdure
hill high mouth of cracked teeth, or
    a bungled sewing, tacks left in.

Slow coil of shadow-dappled waters
    offshore at Argegno—
what are we heading into?
    A theocratic dynasty?
Can I imagine Como carpet-bombed?
No—but I can't imagine 40,000
dead in Iraq either
            —thoughts hurled into
early evening staircased olive trees.
It is my life that ties these granite slopes to
    disenfranchised Florida blacks,
a slim warped pulse as
the hydrofoil breaks for Lezzeno.

Tiny white abandoned house
clutched by vertical bramblework.
Density of mind.
The madness of belief in belief.
For 42% of Americans the devil is incarnate
    and must be flamethrowered out.

Head, motionless belfry
while warring tongues cascade within.
Sweetness of autumn trees,
    scarlet amber canopied,
at the mercy of the mind's agon filters
clotted with greed, immortality.

Cars like toys under the Xmas tree of time,
    first twinkle of the god star
sucking up
          deep sensations of
babyhood now lathered with
    crocodilian pearls.

Don't take me for my belonging,
take me for my hardly being here.

[23 OCTOBER 2004]

53

My innate Indiana tendency is
to tiptoe on a razorblade
and to feel the Presbyterian tingle
masochistically up my spine.

Poetry has been to compel the razored toe tip blade
to hybridize,
to allow an underworld
uprush to fruit through the root twine.

So, who is here at 6 A.M. this morning?

Persephone, kneeling on a pomegranate half,
Eros seated on her shoulder.
I read their hand signs to mean: "Flow! Conceive!
The scisson of the Mother into mother and daughter
is to be found in the abyss of the seed!"

I stooped to inspect the Dionysian upsurge
spreading octopodally through my brain.
I sensed the lost half of myself: my dog, when I was 12,
car-smashed Sparkie, who gave birth to the vine.

Then, in the spectral interior of a cypress, I saw Rilke,
in his death bed, a blackened strawberry,

attended by a kindly bedbug nurse,
his marmalade-soft face still poised in praise—

as the smoking gate moved into presence,
Rainer exchanged verse letters with an 18-year-old Austrian,
Erika Mitterer.
Persephone's verdure and her duration
were now layered into all his transformational gradations.
Not "Here Lies," he wrote,
but "Here Lives," happy to feel the soil
pulse his soot shaft, that cypress affirmation,
overplus of arising
with which the beloved gleams up.

[BELLAGIO, 4 NOVEMBER 2004]

FROM A TERRACE

"We have destroyed Fallujah
so as to convert it"
overheard in the breeze by the massive broken oak.

Sunday lakeside serenity.
People with their skin burned off, hospitals bombed by
an us I bleed in
psychically, my government
completely corrupt.

To be sixty-nine now, "old style"
shot through with fecal sorrow,
bedbugs in my mouth, us-bugs, my whole mouth bugged.

The oak leans into blue rapture
over roily, white-capped
gasoline-turquoise water,
its leaves sort of dribble about in the air.

The carnage cloaked by
television's visibility sterility
—is this less sterile?

Small lichen saucers indented into
hundred year old bark,
noble whorled

wood showing
through, as I would like to.

This asunder-written No to
the interventional might of America,
millions raked into invisible piles,
the 9/11 blowback a drop
in the bucket blood of
Guatemala
Nicaragua
Serbia
Iraq
      How terrible
      to not feel pure
      grief for the
      WTC dead, how
terrible to have to
contextualize to be honest.

Across Lake Como
mountains rest on the waterfold,
slant shadowed rows. They are
mammoth heads with verdant folded eyes,
beautiful, meaningless
                  in
an extinction-tinctured view.

Man driven by hate for what he is,
a lost puppy bowl
mother-licked, father-interfered.

—O breathe and just
enjoy the warmth on writing hand,
the church bell tower below,
its innocent stone crossed by
ravens in the shape of men

    —I can't
    I twist here
mentally gibbeted,
particle of a warrior form,
hell done in my nationality,

the Ho- Ho-
san
ta
cackle-embedded warp in being.

Some axial release holds sway
in the after-
ring of a re-
    immobilizing bell.

[BELLAGIO, 14 NOVEMBER 2004]

ONE IF BY LAND, NONE IF BY VOID

A vertical third eye looks out of, and admits to, paradise, ringed by the hyena graveyard, ringed by the world sty.

At the U.N. Colin Powell said:
   "Vast amounts of chemical weaponry have never accounted for Saddam Hussein.
   Our conservatives in Iraq have stockpiled 500 tons of agents.
   Saddam Hussein's low end, an area nearly five times the size of Manhattan, is solid yellowcake.
   Every statement I deny is buried in unmanned, aerial graves."

That 45 minutes Tony Blair claimed was all Saddam needed is a zone stretching back to the Hammurabi code, and forward to Donald Rumsfeld's *Collected Nonsense* (when you laugh, reader, do not forget that there is a cluster bomblet, waiting, under each of his words, for a child's curious hand).

We are concerned to inform you that mother has loaded her 40-foot red carpet vagina into a Blakean chariot and taken off.

A fashion show dream: sky blue bejeweled plunging décolletage with blood-bubble embroidery. Floor-length silk with a splash of gold pus threadsuns. Americans weaving down the walkway, wearing their terror as part of seasonal design.

Meager nigredo, skinny gold.

The city of Fallujah, returning "home," crawled what was left of their lives like a centipede missing 98 legs.

I wandered the Frida Kahlo Museum, noticing how the clothing of the dead hang, the concave chest areas, the dreadful fullness below.

The chairs like empty beehives. The leg of a papier-mâché skeleton dangling in the breeze, metronome savvy.

This made me think of the cork-screwing dryness of the long adventure through language, how it includes visiting the House of the Dead as well as the children trying to sell chiclets amidst the sluggish midnight weave of cars on Paseo de la Reforma.

Layered Mexico City, whose core is a bicephalic rattlesnake commemorating a woman made pregnant by a feather.

What the Covering Cherub failed to convey, Coatlicue reinforces: you had your uterine moment. Where we imagine tiny fingers once pawing for suck, a garland of lopped off hands crescent Her chest urn.

Bill Clinton as a Nkondi figure, his back bristling with Republican nails and blades.

In Baltimore I got drunk and flipped out. "Where's Caryl?" I shouted, pulling at Caryl's arms. I attempted to protect her in a psychotic fit—we were in Baghdad, under bombardment.

"Rapture" philosophy: the quicker we destroy the reserve of arctic liberality, the quicker we'll get to those black-eyed virgins the suicide-bombers are high on.

Rumor of Bush's Sherman limo heard firing at the faithful packing Penn Ave. Terrorists were reported to be stowed away in the rear axle.

Gorillas in a vaporous *pas de deux* have just line danced through the ward of the legless to remind us of the Swastika Duplex of the heart.

Robert Duncan to Denise Levertov, 1968: "Do we want or dare passionate reality? To suffer the reality of what we are? It is some hovering suspicion of what the passionate reality of Man may be, some hovering suspicion in me of what I have always recognized as true in the testimony of others, that darkens my brooding."

Chances are I'm a Minotaur surrogate,
weaving, at night, an arachnoid adept who jigs about a cordate void,
an anomalous void, orbicular labyrinth.
Chances are, I behead upon being impregnated,
nourishing the just conceived with my brain marrow lunch.
Chances are, I spin-say to myself:
mental war takes place on husk-strewn thread.

The air advertises reality, connecting it,
via respiration, with non-being—
nothing, truly, more noumenal, more depth-resplendent!
But a religious grid, or gradient, an oasis
beyond this worktomb,
verdant, eternal—that, never!

Abdomen-tentacled, I snag
etymological drift, injecting it with literal

breakdown, so as
to turn it, as a threadbaled Thesean,
into drink.

    Thus this spider mind,
this forever warp woof-crossed by never,
this spectral Tenochtitlan,
this Jurassic chandelier.

[FOR JEFF CLARK]

IRAQI MORGUE

Blackened semi-smile
   eyelidlifted turned

rust fur Can't get a
fix on

mangled slab of splintered bone,
stringy red muscles.

Armpit trying to raise
mouth milk,
        eyes
staring at something great.

Eyes like headlights still on
in twisted steel.

0070 64 F 04 is sad,
he's looking up to the right
cheeks bulging.

Some are camouflaged, it seems,
with death labels &
plastic label bags
   —ears show,
    a tooth rip.

Black skin rubble
no eyes   upper teeth
         in death lisp.

Faceless, no, burned to
    a congealed
insectile smear.

Shattered lit
skull rubble through which
one eye blasts.

Maroon head skin
tucked up about its bag shoulder
as if asleep.

What am I looking at?
At horror looking through
an 1899 update:
after the lynch picnic,
the knuckles of Sam Hose displayed
in the window of an Atlanta grocery.

340 04 V 04
nearly all blood.

    Very old man gray
turned head cupped
in death sheet blossom.

A QUESTION FROM GERARDO DENIZ

"Sabes, imbécile, cómo acaban sonando 500 severidades consecutivas?"
They sound like the boots of pallbearers during a parade of flag-draped
    coffins,
a pathetic or inspiring clompathon
depending on the way one feels about
500 refugee tents scattered about the destruction of Fallujah

or a recent dispatch from Dahr Jamail: "an Iraqi friend of mine who is a
doctor in Baghdad told me that when he was in Ramadi yesterday, us soldiers attacked the Anbar Medical School while students were taking their
exams. As he said 'They (us soldiers) smashed the front gates of the school
in a barbaric way using Humvees . . . and terrorized the female students
while arresting two students while they were working on their exams. They
then lay siege to the homes of the dean of the university, along with homes
of lecturers, even though their families were inside.'"

        500 consecutive brutalities.
-5,000 consecutive lies. 50,000 Americans
packing a Colorado Springs evangelical superstructure praying for the
    Rapture.

The sound machines Israelis are experimenting with,
where the drone drives your organs wild and if not turned off tears them
    apart.

The Rumsfeld Doctrine: the absence of evidence is not
    the evidence of absence i.e.,

no weapons of mass destruction found =
immense unfindable quantities of them.

As for climate change: shall we re-sacrifice a few mammoths?

Cartoon of Aztec priests rolling a nuclear bomb up a pyramid,
    ripping out its plutonium heart.

Gerardo, did you know that just 4 percent of the combined wealth of the
225 biggest fortunes (worth a total of $1 trillion) would be enough to pay
for the education, food and basic health care for the planet's entire population?

Believe in the footprint in Mali that contains a village, the dark parts
    animal manure.
Believe that a life, a community, could flourish somewhere, without
    American intervention.

Dahr Jamail (21 June 2005): "'We were tied up and beaten despite being unarmed and having only our medical instruments,' Asma Khamis al-Muhan-
nadi, a doctor who was present during the US and Iraqi National Guard raid
on Fallujah General Hospital told reporters later. She said troops dragged
patients from their beds and pushed them against the wall. 'I was with a
woman in labor, the umbilical cord had not yet been cut,' she said. 'At that
time, a US soldier shouted at one of the National Guards to arrest me and
tied my hands while I was helping the mother to deliver.'"

Anal epoch, millions with their heads up their asses,
patriotizing the shit they see
spread by our junta's appetite.

Tonight the color of the sky is infested, radiant with stealth.
So why do I not stand on my corner with a sign, why do I burrow here?
The trajectory of writing: gouged stone, cuneiform, pen, Microsoft word.
The testimony is caught, a phantom, between the exploding body, news,
   and being here.

My eyes roll back and I see, through the periscope of my skull,
a red churn, fire igniting dew.

Infuriated Botero has for once got it right: the tortured fat of Iraq,
blindfolded, hands tied behind, writhing on Abu Ghraib cell floors.
A bleeding goliath, hanging by his wrists, dressed in pink panties and bra.

I think of you, Gerardo Deniz, in Mexico City,
behind your wall of a skull rack spiked with Coca-Cola shards,
writing your visionary, daffy, meticulous poetry,
snacking on larva bonbons, converting your passing into canine jerks, and,
whenever she struggles up to achieve pedestal,
breaking the legs of glurge.

A FEROCIOUS FOLD

Asger Jorn (1914–1973), I say your Danish name
having met you only seven hours ago
in a COBRA group show
at the Irish Museum of Modern Art.

Consciousness as the hump of a subconscious back.

Jorn, your spatter-driven leach attachings are dabs of a new coherence
bound to your own fate,
steeped in the height of each trapdoor moment.

The cross of man quartered in space,
diapered at the apex of self-display, so as to send the hidden
Adam arsenal
into the subconscious of the worshipper, there to riot
among the still infantile folds of his brain

like an agglomeration of dazed caked bees

like a gourd full of rings made of hardened caterpillars

Bush-locked between Iraq and Katrina,
regard the bottomless shame of cots filled with stomach-exploded
women, legless children,
hospital that looks like an Inquisitional vomitorium

The doctor shot by a marine sniper as he drives home to rest

A girl standing by the roadside with an arm burned to black crust

as the Humvees pass

as the Humvees pass

What Bosch proposed as Apocalypse breaks out, a viral hail,
wherever men are stirred to rampage, or
the theocratic self, infected with a replicating self-justification gnome,
treats all others as Satanic
applause-triggered jokes,
                              the Joker
dashing between the jokes, with his reduction thread,
sewing ear to mouth, that only
the interior may be heard:

the carbonaceous soul of life

the siliceous soul of rock.

DEAD RECKONING

What the Bush junta has destroyed shuts down my mind.
No trope, or, the anti-trope, Atropos, "she who cannot be turned."
For every known horror, there must be
a thousand we do not know about.
News as a palimpsestic labyrinth:
  if you avoid it,
you write a poetry lacking civil reality.
   If you engage it,
you are sucked into full-time media witness/reporting.

What is the nature of this shutdown?
It is the encased feeling of being buried in blur
so voraginous it becomes a liquid mirror
reflecting my erasing angel,
that force in everyone's spectre that disappears
specifics, retains generalities,
shatters attention points, burps drifting stubs.

Recalling years ago, homeless Barbara Mor
spending her days in a Burger King practicing no-mind,

I move, as if by dead reckoning,
through the portico shades of daily judgment,
Hart Crane's tennis racket my paddle.
Pushing my canoe through arctic whiteness,
beer cooler packed with Iraqi hearts.

Overhead, a raptor clutching in its talons
a naked squirming pagan.

Government will have no control over my imagination.
At the very least, the poem will be
a plumb line coiling into cessation,
a momentary dissolution of lunar dread.

Depression conceals what shamans once tooled:
an emptied density
receptive to, gore effaced,
aurochs agency.

Now we are verging on something:
an ice scarp, a ragged file of five menhirs appears,
Noh-ghosts on a bridge between worlds.
Menhir, lighthouse, belted by a sea of diamondback Rapture.
Menhir, nighthouse, the refusing tomb of your long stone blade.

MINOR DRAG

[FOR IAN IRVINE, IN AUSTRALIA]

The body piles at Abu Ghraib,
apple-stacked asses like a gigantic Sadean sexual molecule
male all the way through,
the Caucasian subconscious unleashed on the brown body.

I walk Washtenaw Road,
a pupa in a Hydra-tainted imperial chrysalis.

Controlled demolition of the three Towers.
Controlled demolition of our Constitution.
Controlled demolition of our rights.
Controlled demolition of our environment.
Controlled demolition of our ice.

The missile that penetrated the Pentagon:
The Entry not of Christ
but Pat Robinson into Washington.

It is *Alien* o'clock.
When will the truth explode from Bush's chest?

UNBUCKLED TONGUE

The Last Supper **as** a watermelon feast
each disciple with a tequila-plugged slice
and Jesus already with Isis in his eyes,
be slurped be slain—
to travel as a seed within another's imagination,
arked with lithic freight.

The lunar light dims,
the stone softens. Are we still in
a pagan/Nazarene distillery?
Si, Hart Crane murmurs, from his trench off Tampico,
the stable is a flowchart of Jesus and bison exchange,
yet all takes place in an amphitheater
carved from the rudiments of shamanic protocol.
I hear it in the postponed Ann Arbor sky
as pre-emptive jets pop time.
So it's bolgia within bolgia, a new Comedy—
cosmic structure no longer vortices and trinity,
rather: animating socks, suspenders, a laundry
bag of the mind. Fascism would rinse all to
techno-sheen. CEOs living in platinum grenades
littering planetary shanty-towns.

Note where your first line has taken you,
how each image appears to encyst another,
so that the poem is a mental cave under formation,

the political as the grit in the image water push,
anatomies reconstituting as thresholds,
chalice-shaped cul-de-sacs, the mind anchored and
willy-nilly. Stay aware of the 850 million starving—
such may help keep you honest when the self-censor
purrs: shut up. Unbuckle his tongue from
the door on your heart, show the world-gash
but keep it in your own veins.

Like pinheads in a sunny glade,
JC and his gang are now in round dance,
watched by cranes. Dionysus is near
but so is Ashcroft, while Mother Theresa
cuddles a gigantic gangrenous ear.
Carnival is hardly farewell to the flesh.
In imaginal revision, it is the lambent stampede of
autumn's rash, or Persephone rampant in
the gray November grass. It is the discharge
as the teeth of consciousness sink into
the etymology of gum
releasing depth charges into the mind's ancient hives. Manifesto:
I am here like a scarab rolling my *crottin* through
death's doorway ablaze with billions of golden grubs.
This is the trail I leave,
my wobble weave, analphabetic Lascaux.

THE MAGICAL SADNESS
OF OMAR CACERES

A white road crosses its motionless storm,
vernal pool where frogs live trapped in archaic hail.
I've wasted too much time with moonlight
and now sit gazing through the small hole in my dress at Monday's naked nail.

Manchuria, I feel your invasion!
Suddenly we are ourselves, without brushes, lawn-mowers, or saloons.
I confess the crimes against my monsoon self—
these chess words, slippery with blood,
they are my pistons, my petrol, the fits of memory scrawled in a hulk log.
Cockroaches cross the deck   moving from Picasso to snowman.

The thought lost to the eyes of a unicorn reappears in a dog's bark.
Dressed in resistance, I laud the most important leader in the United States:
Mickey Mouse, legislator of urban alcohol adieu.
My courtesan instructs me in the wrecked balcony of her arms.
The idol? A chessboard of truffles and snow.
Unlike comrade Huidobro, I'm a whittled id,
a city hall boss standing on prison steps,
thriving like a burnt out sun, a sun which never imagined a lamp.
O summation of Chile! A man loves only his obscure wife.

To run with the nectar, to bypass alarm.
Is not joy somehow canopic?
What moves in the air: ways that are not the way,

the whey of snow, way of the flayed flake.
My slash is yours, riptides amassing.
O Chilean summation! I poke into the moon's watery lace.
Between sequitur and non sequitur falls the imagination.
"There is grandeur in this life, with its several powers."
Spare the gestures. Nothing for show.
I am neither aft nor fore, nor foreafter,
nor ever to be afterforementioned again.

I hear Neruda—he's a langoustine of a man,
a violet maiden in multicolored fleece,
both hands paralyzed from swatting political lice.
Neruda! A swiller of a gale, a snood disguised as a church,
rutabaga in cleats, something found on the beach which,
as you fondle it, urinates in your heart. Neruda,
what is truly to be found under his tray of forceps and sledges?

Passing mons Veneris clouds.
The translucence of human flesh.
Ceremonial lenses made of ice, brought down from Andean peaks.
A rainbow defective in a single hue.
The spider *Dolomedes urinator* which runs simultaneously in two worlds.
The sound of air in a cave.
Sensation of longing for an eclipse powerful enough to darken death.
Changes in the light initiated by a stranger's arrival
—Chilean marvels, equal to the Surreal.

I prepared. Waited to be called.
Cut logs. Laid a hearth. Burned my valentines.

Visited the Incan adoritories on Mount Llullaillaco.

Examined the grave goods of The Prince of Mount Plomo.

Which is to say: I prepared. Set the caldron boiling,

spliced postcards from Isla Negra with photos of infants left out in the snow.

Mastered myself. Arrived in Harar with only 10 camels.

Sketched each waterfall. Took out no personal ads.

I faced fear, then clarity, then power.

Tonight I have a meeting with the last enemy of the man of knowledge.

In his uncorked left testicle, it has been raining for years.

TRAIN DREAM

In the station the trains were dreaming,
defenseless, without locomotives, asleep.

Hesitantly I entered at dawn:
I went about searching for secrets,
things lost in the carriages, in the stale odor of the journey.
Among the departed bodies
I felt how alone I was in the stationary train.

The air was dense, a block of disheartened
conversations, of fugitive languor.
Lost souls on trains like keys
without locks, fallen under the seats.

Women passengers from the south laden
with bouquets and chickens,
maybe they were murdered,
maybe they returned and wept,
maybe they consumed the carriages
with the fire of their carnations,
maybe I am traveling alongside them,
maybe the steam of the journeys,
the wet rails . . . maybe everything is alive
in the motionless train
and I a sleeping passenger
unfortunately alert.

I was seated and the train was moving
inside my body, annihilating my frontiers,
suddenly it was the train of my childhood,
the smoke of daybreak,
happy and bitter summer.

There were other trains which were fleeing,
cars crammed with sorrow
as if packed with asphalt,
thus did the motionless train press on
during a morning that was increasingly
painful for my bones.

I was alone in the lonesome train,
but not only was I alone,
many solitudes had congregated there
hoping to travel like the poor on the platforms.
And I, in the train, like lifeless smoke,
with so many ungraspable beings,
overwhelmed by so many deaths,
felt myself lost on a journey in which
nothing was moving but my weary heart.

[AFTER "SUEÑOS DE TRENES,"
BY PABLO NERUDA,
ESTRAVAGARIO, 1958]

SURVEILLANT VEILS

[FOR ANDREW JORON]

I reached through art to touch ensouled stone,
a once
fully-embraced ever
now ensouled in never.

Organically, I am encased in never.
Creatively, I neverize
to reconstitute ever.

All the elements of this wall,
according to George Oppen, have come
from eternity.

Why, when I look at that thought, do I see
a Malawi prison floor covered with
bedraggled men,

or recall
the sorrow charged and twisted face of an Iraqi
clawing at her 9-year-old son's tiny coffin?

It is good that her ululation
makes me ashamed of my own fulfillment,

good too that first light can still be imagined,
suppurant as it is
with the wounds in that child's box.

There is rage in the body's sequences—

cancer cells, immortalizing, divide
until they kill their host.

Eternity is pregnant with
the mortal tern.

IMPROVISATIONS OFF
WATERCOLORS BY
MARY HEEBNER

The glacier in the sky, mind the tip of it.

Like a page from *Finnegan's Wake* given to prison guards
or the Apse in Lascaux where, for perhaps the first time,
the volley of animal life
went into astro-boogie with the night sky.

To discover the stone in urine.
Or felicity, watching Bush strangle Tenet with his medal cord.
If blue is darkness made visible,
is not blackness the void made tangible?
Starlight is almost flesh.

It is the glacier's lower body that most engages me,
the subconscious of a god
enchased, mind as a fern rooted in pile driver clouds.

I watched the Extraterrestrials emerge from their Superbowl locker.
The quarterback had a single eye in the vertical log of his head,
the fullback a bonfire for hair, three tiny eyes stapled in his skull.
Or were these sky folk, kicked out of their storm,
a projection of my desire
to install the uncanny in the fortress of power?

There's a dark blue wound peristaltic in the sky's white simmer,
a caterpillar attempting to strum a harp,
larvae itching to emerge from the boil of war.

Unplug my ears, Tiresias,
I want to hear the snakes sprout from Medusa's fontanel,
like souls popping through purgatorial crust.

Sky, great screen showing Never and Its Analogues—
silver flotillas that make me hear
Bud Powell playing "It never entered my mind,"
hesitating, from chord to chord, as if each bloom
vanished as he burgeoned.
In the cyanotics of blue, sky performs
the mysteries and horrors of the earth.

An immense dog phallus bends over, grinning sleepily,
its tongue hanging from its crotch. When I look again,
an infant is extending salamander fingers . . .

■

Eight cubes circumambulate a lizard head
the eyes of which are closed, mouth clenched—
eight pilgrims, eight hyena clouds
spilling into peach, like panels of Little Nemo in Dreamland, 1906,
elasticizing according to the dreamer's needs.

These cubes revolve to put pressure on
the Kaba or cubic breast
with black nipple cornerstone to be kissed—

eight million pilgrims in line before a pyramid,
its shaft leading to an interior crypt
where the King, an eternal infant, is forever setting forth on
the Road of Awe.

Under the King is the Queen,
under the crypt a cave! I evoke Le Combel,
its manganese-daubed pod-shaped stalactites,
the 17,000-year-old breast foliage of the most ancient
Tree of Life.
                    The breast, the part of myself
I lost at birth. Along the milk path
the shaman lopes, along its subincision.
The Milky Way: mother and son in copulation stuck.

Mens' lives are shadowed by this primal seam.

Areola complex, twin of the nipple ring our eyes enchase.

The breast as a curving white screen.
Are all actors placental specters?

"The prototype of all bad objects by its absence"—
but is it ever absent? Are not all lost objects breast-charged?

In my dream I descended by umbilical dropline
into a hut of humming
love-mad bees. It became a candy house
with a long-nosed witch, dugs reaching to her whirlpool
groin where I saw Kore disappear . . .

Every daughter the disjoined continuation of her mother,
the hole that eating the apple makes in the self.

Paradise as placenta. Blood round table,
our mother on all fours, headless, our breast-planed mother,
glabrous andesite, here as never,
     gravid,   ever her.

                    ■

Panther-headed cloud man in orange recline,
what can you tell me about Neruda's sleep?

"A spoonful of god immensity
has gradually worn away my star.
The rusty fire in the snow-polar blue
reminds me of every woman I have grazed.
Each point of focus, even a maggot's shadow
or the quiver of a blood-ravenous autumn,
is the inverted realm of a black sun
crossed by the ethnospheric mantle of a golden sun.
Everything we see is X-rayed with a fragmentary,
fleeting human body, a torso of salt-stained

roses, oily spine lightning, blackened by
freed shadows, darter midnights.
At what appear to be edges, there is only entrance into
the vale of flash-back, flash-
forward, the unknown Six-Wired Bird of Paradise,
the Long-Beaked Echidna,
the Golden-Mantled Tree Kangaroo,
the Smoky Honeyeater,
the Microhylid Tree Frog.
Each a vast cosmic canyon, a rainbow tornado,
a thigh of ciphers launched from a groin of
towering pillars of cool gas."

In Neruda's sleep, the surf rains like sand
through impenetrable blue. Light is an echo,
stacked shores a perfect wall
he runs his hand across, then reads in palm:
delta, orchard, Southern Cross. He contemplates
stepping back into existence. Cancer. Pinochet.

Revolution at best breaks up the ice over the abyss.

Awakening we see a partially-cleared sky
to realize we are still inside the spacious cave of the dream.

■

The Torso Nebula, a celestial essence of
great presence, beaten blue, burnished white,

charred, cored,

                recalling Robert Duncan's

The Torso   Passages 18

"my hand in your hand   seeking   the locks, the keys"

Holding Duncan's Hand I first called *Lachrymae Mateo*,

told Duncan objected, I retitled, with Crane in mind.

And now this blistered cosmogonic male-scape,

black holes like battered eyes. Hart Crane beaten to the extent

Siqueiros could not look at him while he painted him

and asked him to lower his head.

                          I am glad for my

homosexual dreams, they display a camaraderie

I feel is adhesive; they link me, however feebly,

     to Whitman's vista—

in Mary Heebner's vision the struggle of two Titans

makes up a nebular fury, they go at each other

as the nature of divided man.

                   What depths of sorrow

do we never plumb? As if my question might travel to

that point where

our collective inability to accept dying

deigned to

         destroy the earth.

■

This waterfall is a glacial
angel waver, of
charcoal, limestone, an icicle
anchored in the upspring of my forever-
eager and hopeful
female form. This pit plunges
through her, yet look—
she incorporates the ashen meal, breaks out
with the pox of destruction,
for it is all polysemous,
not only the nation but the soul
and the poem are involved in the event.

Waterfall dropping as exclamation mark,
as navel point ending.
                    In my storm mind,
lurid war news, the fragments of old myths . . .
Hacked genitals, surf ignite,
a scream rises from a terrified 13-year-old Nigerian girl's
foaming mouth. There is no Venus here.
I paste in the past because, like this scarred
angel, it is implanted,
viable, a charged depth,
coarse with smoke, the traceries,
of the holocaust I remember,
and of the one, a few thousand miles to the left of my eye,
now digging in. Darfur. Congo. And,
shellacked with liquid flame, Iraq.

I am confronted with the moral disease
Baudelaire cut into, the tumor of the self.
As an American, it is now impossible to look at something and,
as we used to say, see it for itself.
A desert beast? Of sorts, the planetary manticore
out there is a film I project, willy-nilly,
as it hums behind my eyes, its cradle song.

—And yet the god face lines in Villarrica's snow leathery summit, the sea of
   blue fog islanding the summits beyond . . .
The long strips of turmeric-colored *sari* cloth drying in Jaipur sunlight . . .
Like a broken mirror, the thin ice of the Baltic reflecting the feeble light
   of Finnish winter . . .
A surge of brown, white-headed Hereford cows crossing Chimehuin
   River . . .
The coral reefs under New Caledonia's turquoise lagoons, poisoned by
   nickel extraction run-off . . .
A rusting, sand-sodden wrecked ship on Namibia's Skeleton Coast . . .
Kakadu National Park marshes, their interlocked avocado and red
   earth-colored formations . . .
The "petting pools" at Puerto Vallarta, where red-life-jacketed tourists
   touch stressed, obese dolphins . . .
Wind-scalloped, frothy white dune sand in the midst of a deep green Fraser
   Island forest . . .
Bubbling yellow sulfur red iron oxidic green arsenic in the volcanic
   steaming waters off New Zealand's North Island . . .
Standing Belgian horses, their late-afternoon elongated pike-like khaki
   shadows . . .
A three-mile green salt and pepper horde of fifty billion locusts ravaging
   Madagascar pastures . . .

> "one lone Indian
> fishing in the river at the bottom of
> the Barranca del cobre"

An estuary crocodile moving through a Buccaneer Archipelago mangrove
     swamp . . .
The Genbaku Dome, the only building shell in Hiroshima to survive the
     August 6, 1945, atomic bomb . . .
Hiram Bingham's tight hairpin climbing road looping toward Machu
     Picchu . . .
The pear glaze stains in the bottom of my soaking sautée pan, as captivating,
     as beautiful . . .
Lake Argentino's bluish-green glacier cream . . .
Petra's pink and yellow sandstone temples . . .
The moss-carpeted lava streams of Lakagigar . . .
The dead alive domes of Purnululu, tiger-stripe layered silica and lichen,
     fissured, forced up,
equals, on a scale I have yet to plumb,
each an end point shadow, elders possessing the strata of languages not to
     be passed on . . .

WHOLESOME

It was like starting out, to build,
with only libations and words, a house.

In this nothereal atmosphere,
the result arrived before the process:
an archangelic beehive with roller coasters
transporting ark wagons of animals and fish,
jetting them onto a tundra
where glass trees buzzed with exiled bees
fueled by the bellows in the gut-vaults of a wasp queen
buried in
the mud at the bottom of
a landless sea.
                    Thus not a beehive
but a pandemonic wasp nest,
crossing escalators bearing centipede tabernacles
ascended descending, while
in the background, a haberdashery,
managed by a lamb-faced moth, displayed
caterpillar gloves and suspenders from eel-traps
still wriggling.

Upshot of an hour with the poetry of Peter Redgrove.

∎

We all start out as somebody else, somebody we do not know. We are born as an enigma, of which we are unaware. We are also unaware that we seem to come out of nothing, since we do not know for sure if any root of self existed before.

They called me Sonny, because my first hair was orange. They were afraid I was going to be a redhead. No one in the family knew what to do with a redhead.

I hardly knew my childhood. Flashes of play, at a white picket fence, which I held onto at eleven, screaming that I wanted to go to Jeannie Woodring, two years older than me, next door. The holding onto those pickets, that was something!

I was so hot I could've melted the pickets, and that repressed heat, boy, it has been with me forever.

■

For centuries, it seems, Redgrove lay, scissorlike,
in meditative intercourse, with Penelope's shuttle
(the red grove in which his peter
luxuriated), like rocks hooded with blood,
two axles of the abyss,
flexing their granular gills . . .

                         Hovering over,
I watched their energy manifest as musical swoops,
fly mica eighth notes, bluebell semen whole.
I saw a spirit-pass enweb between them,

a kind of nectar winking with shimmering chimera,
a magical child shuddering mauve lightning.
As fearless as her console, and in constant transformation,
it played between them, undulating to some heresiarch's
wand, determined to move English poetry
out of its lavender kilts to a maggot-keen anointment.

I saw their conjunction as a mandala to steer by,
a mandala of renewal and centered life, with ten mahogany spokes,
a nub of brass, a great round tree
pointing a route.

Where did you get your cobra parasol?
I made it out of the skin of my own split umbilicus.

Are you a womb passenger still?
Yes, in the sense that this
dangles, like a parachutist, from angelic cords,
attached to a pileus that goes back to *amanita muscaria* and
the patagium of flying squirrels.

In a cradle scene, performed on a Muybridge zoöpraxiscope,
Jesus recognized his sister JIsis.
The he-fury in our being is fueled by the charcoal razor pyres of
    revolutions that have failed.
Love for everyone revealed as a never-cresting orgasm.
Hate boiled to a neutrality, then retrogressed.

Responsible imagination posed against that phyloxera of the spirit:
    political hope.
A wasp tolled the crucifix.

The oldest of thrills is still to bloom
    and hold.

COMBINED OBJECT

Listening to Caryl sleep,
thinking of the cross-hatching in the 7-mile verticality of her living,
the Challenger Deep
as her mind makes its way across the 40,000-mile mid-ocean ridge,
across abyssal plains and canyons in tree-shaped networks,
across the hadal trench off Peru containing the oldest water in the world,
her young life, which she remembers so keenly,
like a die tumbling among arabesques of leafy sea dragons with seaweed wings
trailing kelp blends, green clouds pouring
from the sides of wounded fish, millions of image trains,
I am on one, looking down at the stratified trains below,
one called Venus's-flower-basket, the passengers:
shrimp, crabs, worms, and clams. Multiple water spindles containing
water fairy proms, high school friends being reborn,
I am following the course of her sleep
through sea pastures of whirring diamond saws,
under a cowl of pelican eels,
in full flight, astride the thorax of a four-winged flyer
she carries away with her, in her trailing skirts,
a web filled with tiny men, drowned islands, radiolarian ooze,
at 800 feet, only the deepest, blackest blue,
the ocean of her sleep breaks over me, like light gravel,
sensation of being in a horse's mouth, a deeper breathing is forming—
the infinite, far from being a suburb of the gods,
is an eternal surpassing, removed from any essential halt.
I see her standing before a glass stairway, a Jacob's ladder
with more steps than she could ever climb in three lifetimes,

they disappear like bubbles in champagne,

now she is struggling against

suctions and pulls, against stretched webs, against curving spidery legs,

she breaks free—what nightmare did she just slip?—

she becomes navigation itself, shining with a pure white flame,

passing over foaming ditches, wheeling ravines,

I imagine her retinue: dwarf plankton,   flamingo tongues,

coccoliths giving the water a milk glow,   bristlefooted worms

patterned with colored rosettes,   arrow worms like fine threads of glass,

pteropods with winged feet,   salmon-pink winged slugs,

salps like little barrels, pulsating, a mouth at each end—

out of the warm, dimly lit, dilute broth of a shallow Silurian sea

a jointed-legged proto-scorpion,   ancestor of all on land.

How do without a head? How present all edges of the body

equally to the outside world? A poem without subject,

all parts of which surprise and interlock, a poem with twenty centers,

all muscular and avid, each word dense, full in itself, a nest,

a sound of wood crackling in the fireplace, a shiver without skin,

each word an outpost, a courier, monkey words

feeling the earthquake coming before I do.

Going through myself,   is it her heart that I am hearing?

—she gasps—silence—rebreathes   ka   ka   ka   ka

suddenly, she is other than herself,

rake tines rise from her brow projecting brain energy into the atmosphere,

impaling celestial hexes, they glow pale blue in the dark

like thin upraised arms; I pass slowly through them,

standing in my Protestant canoe, alone, stiff, an erection curving

from a golden pubic beard—behind my back,

the Absolute, straight as a wall.

I am possessed by a sole idea: that snow is ceaselessly falling

obliquely through all of us, on each flake
the population of the Beyond cluster
like minute beardless seals, or albino cougars,
spherical, knots of unearthly calm
sailing on an invisible current. As my monoxylon
sinks slowly into dead space, the dark is flecked with one-winged birds,
with barkless trees, and I also see the full squalor of the sea,
the rubbish of a thousand boats daily fished up, winnowed,
and thrown straight back—crushed into the netted haul
the new mermaid, limbs twisted among dogfish, whiting, and plaice,
a deflated life-sized sex doll, hermit-crabs inside
her red-rimmed mouth. O sea layered into my dreams,
the daily rewound trash,   visitations of the dead,   Tenochtitlan
thoroughfares,   extra-terrestrial spider queens,
cork-screwing flights through kaleidoscopic barriers
to land by a nightstand and be watched by
two swans,   who are being watched by
two ocelots,   who are being watched by two snakes,   watched by
sixteen triangles,   watched by countless staring eyes.
Cessation of the mirage of the finite,
illusory conviction that anything concluded exists—
call it re-embarkation, call it a multiple leaving.
I have for shade a whole spread of hyena shadow.
I am my own ground, slashed, a wild sea of ground.
There is a silent breaking of waves,   spots of light,   sensation of fissure,
a flowing furrow,   I see Caryl gliding through
the infinite little curlicues in its flanks,
when I graze her I graze a deep pit of joy.

"AN ALCHEMIST WITH ONE EYE ON FIRE": This essay was originally a talk written for the May 2002 International Poetry Conference at the Bibliothèque Nationale Mitterand in Paris.

"LIFE IN THE FOLDS": The painter Matta's brief appearance at the beginning of "Nocturnal Veils" is developed in this poem. The title, "Life in the Folds," is a translation of Henri Michaux's *La vie dans les plis* (the title of a collection of his poems), which I re-encountered at a Matta show in the Malingue art gallery in Paris, June 1 (my birthday), 2004. I spent several happy hours at this show, which included paintings from 1936 to 1944. After a half hour or so of looking, I began to write rapidly in a notebook, drifting around the gallery, from painting to painting (or drawing to drawing), letting Matta's metaphoric deep space constructions, which evoke the cosmos as well as the recesses of the mind, impinge and flush out language. A couple of my phrases—"convict of light" and "panic suction of the sun" —are translations of Matta titles.

Matta is indescrible in the way that late Arshile Gorky is, and is thus a delicious challenge to articulate, since any words one finds seem to come out of a collision between one's own tapped subconscious and his anti-illustrative forms.

"AN ENIGMATIC SIGNIFIER": The poem makes use of material to be found in Jean LaPlanche's *Seduction, Translation, Drives* (Institute of Contemporary Arts, London, 1992), specifically the essay "The Drive and Its Object-source: its fate in the transference."

"LAURA": The James Hillman quote comes from his book *The Force of Character* (Ballantine Books, 1999), specifically from the chapter "Return."

"SAMPERI'S DIAGRAM": The poet Frank Samperi's (1933–1991) major work is a trilogy made up of *The Prefiguration, Quadrifariam,* and *Lumen Gloriae,* all published by Mushinsha-Grossman, in 1971 and 1973. Station Hill brought out a selected poems by Samperi, *Spiritual Necessity,* edited by John Martone, in 2003. I knew Frank both in NYC and in Kyoto, and published his *Crystals* as a Caterpillar Book (1967), as well as some of his poems in *Caterpillar* magazine. He is a unique figure in American poetry, whose force field gravitated totally around Dante.

"FOR GUSTAF SOBIN": The poet, essayist, and novelist Gustaf Sobin's (1935–2005) last book of poetry, *The Places as Preludes* (Talisman, 2005), perhaps his finest, appeared immediately after his death, as did a festschrift, edited by Andrew Joron and Andrew Zawacki, *Miracle of Measure Ascendant*, also published by Talisman. Gustaf moved to Provence in the 1960s, finding his true home there near the poet René Char, whom he translated. Caryl and I last visited him in the summer of 2004. He took us to Char's birthplace, his last home, and to his tomb which Gustaf tended conscientiously for years, clipping and watering the bushes that semi-encircled it. While we were standing there, a strange creature appeared out of thin air. I jotted in my notebook:

> *At the tomb of*
> *René Char*
> *a humming sect*
> *without inn or*
> *bird.*

"NORA'S TRANSMISSION": My requiem for my dear friend, the painter Nora Jaffe (1928–1994) is to be found in *From Scratch* (Black Sparrow Press, 1998), along with notes on Jaffe's art by Adrienne Rich and Robert Kelly. In "Nocturnal Veils," when I impulsively asked, "Nora, how is it where you are?" I got an earful from a dimension I had not planned to visit. Then in the spring of 2003, this Nora voice returned and over several weeks offered me the material to be found in this "transmission." I was not actually "hearing voices." Feeling that Nora wanted to speak with me again, I opened myself to what I took to be what she had to say.

"AUTUMN 2004": The "Cain's right leg . . ." quotation comes from Dan Baum's article, "The Casualty," in the March 8, 2004, issue of *The New Yorker*.

"COMO—BELLAGIO 4:22 P.M.": this poem, and the two that follow it, were written at the Rockefeller Study Center at Bellagio, on Italy's Lake Como, in November 2004, while I was in residency there to study Hieronymus Bosch's triptych, *The Garden of Earthly Delights*. I discovered a copy of a translation of Rilke's verse letter exchange with Erica Mitterer in the Study Center library.

"ONE IF BY LAND, NONE IF BY VOID": The Robert Duncan quote is from *The Letters of Robert Duncan and Denise Levertov*, Stanford University Press, 2004, Letter

#418. Beginning with "Chances are, I am a Minotaur surrogate . . ." the poem becomes an improvisation on—one could almost say a translation of—my translation of César Vallejo's poem, "A lo mejor, soy otro," which can be found in *The Complete Poetry of César Vallejo*, University of California Press, 2006.

"IRAQI MORGUE": The source for this poem is "The Face of War," an album containing photos taken on November 19, 2004, by the American military, of dead men in Fallujah. This album is to be found on Dahr Jamail's Iraq Dispatches site: www.dahrjamailiraq.com.

"A QUESTION FROM GERARDO DENIZ": The poet Gerardo Deniz (Madrid, 1934) has lived in Mexico City for many years and, in my opinion, has written the most engaging poetry in Mexico after Octavio Paz. A capably-translated selection of his poetry by Monica de la Torre may be found in *poemas / poems*, published by Ditoria/Lost Roads Publishers in 2000.

"THE MAGICAL SADNESS OF OMAR CÁCERES": See Eliot Weinberger's essay "Omar Cáceres," in *Karmic Traces* (New Directions, 2000). According to Weinberger, Cáceres is one of many significant and forgotten twentieth century Latin American poets, and one who is known only by a collection of fifteen poems published by his brother in Chile in 1934. Weinberger translates, in his essay, one of these poems, and this translation, along with the bits of information on the poet, moved me to write my own poem in the voice of Omar Cáceres. Since then, I have found out the Editiones El Tucán de Virginia in Mexico City brought out an edition of Cáceres' *Defensa del Idolo* in 1996. In the second issue of the translation magazine *Circumference*, there is a translation of Cáceres' poem, "Opposite Anchors," by Monica de la Torre.

"IMPROVISATIONS OFF WATERCOLORS BY MARY HEEBNER": The Santa Barbara-based painter Mary Heebner incorporates papers, powdered pigments, and "anything that will dissolve in water" into her mixed media pieces. Her inspirations are global, including the temple ruins of Southeast Asia, the Ice Age cave imagery of southwest France, and Iceland's volcanic landscape. I did my "improvisations" while looking at computer print-outs of watercolors, along with her lovely contributions to *On the blue shore of silence/Poems of the sea* by Pablo Neruda, translated by Alastair Reid (HarperCollinsRayo, 2003).

"EARTH FROM ABOVE": Based on photos from Yann Arthus-Bertrand's book,

Earth from Above (Harry N. Abrams, 2003). The quotation at the bottom of page 92 consists of the last three lines of Charles Olson's *West* (Goliard Press, 1966).

"WHOLESOME": Peter Redgrove (1932–2003), who lived much of his adult life in Cornwall, England, like Antonin Artaud, always stimulates me to write while reading him. Last fall, I took *My Father's Trapdoors* (Cape Poetry, 1994) into a local coffee shop and after an hour of reading, set the book aside and wrote the first section of "Wholesome." Redgrove's feel for nature is even more receptive than Rilke's; his sensual imagination is unparalleled in twentieth-century British poetry. With his wife and loadstone Penelope Shuttle, he wrote *The Wise Wound: Menstruation and Everywoman* (Penguin, 1979). To my knowledge, this was one of the first books to recover and explore menstrual mythology (concisely detailed several years later in Barbara G. Walker's *The Woman's Encyclopedia of Myths and Secrets*, Harper & Row, 1984). I carried Redgrove books with me while doing research on Upper Paleolithic cave imagery in the 1980s and '90s. Two of my favorite books of his are *The Weddings at Nether Powers* and *The Man Named East* (both Routledge & Kegan Paul, 1979 and 1985). There is a fascinating interview with him by Philip Fried in *The Manhattan Review*, Summer, 1983.

"COMBINED OBJECT": The poem makes use of materials from *Abyss* by C. P. Idyll (Thomas Y. Crowell Company, 1964), the paintings of Henri Michaux, and David Ball's translations in *Darkness Moves: an Henri Michaux Anthology, 1927– 1984* (University of California Press, 1994).

A C K N O W L E D G M E N T S

Some of these poems (and the introductory essay) appeared, occasionally in different forms, in the following magazines and newspapers: *American Poetry Review*, *Action Restreinte* (Paris), *Alligator* (Belgium), *The Ann Arbor News*, *Arson*, *Brooklyn Rail*, *Denver Quarterly*, *Fence*, *House Organ*, *Hunger*, *Milk*, www.millish.com, *New American Writing*, *Poésie* (Paris), *Vanitas*, *The Writer's Chronicle*, *Ygdrasil* (Canada), *Damn the Caesars*, *Talisman*, *Call*, *No: A Journal of the Arts*, and *Cipher Journal*.

"The Magical Sadness of Omar Cáceres" was selected by Paul Muldoon for *The Best American Poetry 2005* (Scribners).

"Nocturnal Veils" first appeared in *Unarmed Chapbook #3* (St. Paul, 2003).

"For Gustaf Sobin" first appeared in *Miracle of Measure Ascendant: A Festschrift for Gustaf Sobin* (Talisman, 2005).

"Nocturnal Veils" and "The Magical Sadness of Omar Cáceres" appeared in *Everwhat* (Zasterle Books, La Laguna-Tenerife, Canary Islands, 2003).

CLAYTON ESHLEMAN was born in Indianapolis, Indiana, in 1935. The author of more than twenty-five books, including fourteen collections of poetry, he is the recipient of the National Book Award, the Landon Translation Prize from the Academy of American Poets, a Guggenheim Fellowship, and several fellowships from the National Endowment of the Arts and the National Endowment for the Humanities. He is also a masterly translator, especially from the Spanish of Neruda and Vallejo and the French of Artaud and Césaire. In 2003, Wesleyan University Press published Eshleman's *Juniper Fuse: Upper Paleolithic Imagination and the Construction of the Underworld*, the fruit of a thirty-year investigation into the origins of image-making and poetry via the Ice Age painted caves of Southwestern France. In 2006 the University of California will publish Eshleman's translation of *The Complete Poetry of César Vallejo*. In 2007 Black Widow Press will publish *Archaic Design*, a collection of his recent essays and prose poems. Eshleman's writings and translations have been published in over five hundred literary magazines and newspapers throughout the world. A professor emeritus of English at Eastern Michigan University, he continues to live in Ypsilanti with his wife, Caryl.

Roof Slates & Other Poems by Pierre Reverdy
translated with an introduction by Mary Ann Caws & Patricia Terry
[FORTHCOMING]

Essential Poems & Writings of Joyce Mansour: A Bilingual Anthology
translated with an introduction by Serge Gavronsky
[FORTHCOMING]

MODERN POETRY SERIES

An Alchemist with One Eye on Fire
Clayton Eshleman

Archaic Design
Clayton Eshleman
[FORTHCOMING]

NEW POET SERIES

Signal from Draco: Poems of Mebane Robertson
[FORTHCOMING]

AND MORE ...

www.blackwidowpress.com